101 PREGNANCY QUESTIONS YOU DIDN'T THINK TO ASK YOURSELF

A Q&A FOR EVERY PREGNANT AND EXPECTING MOM TO ENSURE A SAFE BIRTH AND HEALTHY NEWBORN BABY

ELIZABETH NEWBOURNE

CONTENTS

14 Baby Essentials Every Mom Must Have...

This checklist includes:

- 14 ESSENTIALS THAT YOU DIDN'T KNOW YOU NEEDED FOR YOUR LITTLE ONE AND YOURSELF
- ITEMS WHICH WILL MAKE BEING A MAMA BEAR EASIER
- WHERE YOU CAN PURCHASE THESE ITEMS AT THE LOWEST PRICE

The last thing you want to do is be unprepared and unequipped to give your little one an enjoyable and secure environment to grow up in. It is never too late to prepare for this!

To receive your free Mommy Checklist,
visit the link or scan the QR code below:

https://purelypublishing.activehosted.com/f/1

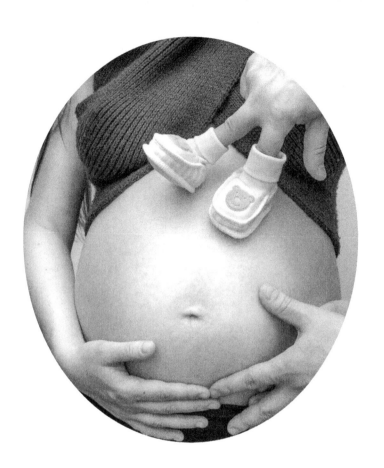

Watch out, baby on board! A positive pregnancy test can turn your life upside down—even if you and your partner were trying to conceive. It's as if seeing those two pink lines trigger an emotional roller coaster. One second you feel overjoyed at the prospect of being a mom, then you'll all of a sudden start questioning your ability to raise a happy and healthy child.

There's no doubt that your life changes drastically when a little human starts to grow in you. From the moment you find out you're pregnant, a lot of questions will need answering. Although most of the things you're wondering about are serious, some more funny questions may pop into your head. "Will my partner's penis poke my baby in the head during sex?" is one of those awkward questions that most pregnant women can't help but ask.

In this book, there are no stupid questions—but there are some truly hilarious ones mixed in with the important things you need answers to. Some of the questions may go through your mind early on but won't end up mattering at all as you grow in your pregnancy. For example, you may want to know if you'll poop when you push during labor. I can promise you that will be the last thing on your mind when you're giving birth—you may even not notice if you do have an oopsie. But there's no harm in knowing the answer anyway, right? It will help control the pregnancy anxiety that appeared out of nowhere!

One of the main things pregnant women want to know is: will this hurt my baby? Everyday activities turn into questions; "Can I eat this?" "Is this body lotion safe for my growing baby?" "Can I sleep in this position?" Overthinking is a big part of pregnancy, especially if you're expecting your first child. Every new mom starts off knowing absolutely nothing about being pregnant, and that is why it is okay to ask. It's also usually first-time moms that come up with chuckle-worthy questions. Thank you, humor is an excellent distraction from the swollen feet, back-ache, and general discomfort that goes hand-in-hand with pregnancy.

Interestingly enough, studies show that 50% of patients don't remember the information their doctor discussed during the consultation (Kessels, 2003). It may be even more difficult for pregnant women to recollect what their doctor told them—it's as if their pregnancy anxiety and haywire emotions wipe their memory entirely. And when their doctor wants to know if they have any questions, they forget what they wanted to ask. But that's no problem, you'll have 101 of your questions answered after you read this book. I know you probably have closer to 300 question marks floating around in your head but we have to start somewhere, and there's no better place than answering 101 of the most-asked pregnancy questions.

1. CAN I EAT NORMAL FOOD?

*F*ood, glorious food—especially when you're eating for two, right? The good news is, apart from the exclusion of a handful of foods (raw eggs, sushi, organ meats, etc.), you can continue eating normally. There's no pregnancy-specific diet you have to follow, but the more nutritious food you eat, the better for you and your growing baby.

Of course, there will be times when 'normal' is the last word you'll use to describe what's in your mouth. Just over 80% of pregnant women will experience cravings at one point or another. But where some will send their husband to buy ice cream to dip their pickles into, others want to eat very peculiar things. Soap, toothpaste, dirt—the list goes on. I have female friends who are too embarrassed to share their cravings with anyone and I understand why. Telling the world you feel like eating a cigarette will most probably raise some eyebrows.

So, although you're allowed to eat normal foods, be ready to add some unusual delicacies to your menu.

2. CAN I BEND OVER, REACH, OR CARRY THINGS?

Yes, you can, but be careful. Normal, everyday movements aren't a cause for concern; it's when you overdo it that it becomes a problem. Bending more than 20 times a day or lifting objects continuously, may increase your chances of miscarriage or preterm delivery (Juhl et al., 2013). You're also at higher risk of injury when you're pregnant since your posture and balance are affected.

Then there's the issue of the pregnancy hormones. Believe me, if you thought your hormones played havoc on your mood and body when you weren't pregnant, you're in for a surprise. Your hormones when pregnant will affect everything—and I mean everything; your hair, nails, weight, mood, sleep, and ligaments and joints (Marnach et al., 2003).

It makes sense why you're more accident-prone at this time, so best to leave the heavy lifting to someone else.

3. WILL SEX POKE THE BABY?

Are you asking for a friend? Just kidding, I know it's not only the husbands who worry about their sex lives—or lack thereof—during pregnancy. Well, you'll both be happy to read that having sex is absolutely fine. Not only will your husband's penis not get anywhere near your baby's head, but your baby won't even know.

Furthermore, your doctor may even tell you to have more sex! If your due date has come and gone, your doctor may recommend you and your hubby go for a twist in the sheets to induce labor. That's because sperm contains prostaglandins—a hormone that stimulates the uterus to contract (Carbone et al., 2019).

4. WON'T GOING NUMBER ONE SO MANY TIMES HURT MY BLADDER?

You'll be spending a lot of time in the loo, especially in the first trimester. But, later on, this need to urinate frequently will most likely reappear as the space inside your uterus gets smaller and your baby starts to press on your bladder. It's annoying, but not dangerous. It's actually much better for your bladder to let it out than hold it in (Science Alert, 2018). You're also more likely to get a urinary tract infection if you hold in your urine.

5. CAN DRINKING MILK IMPROVE MY BABY'S COMPLEXION?

There's nothing you can do to make your baby's skin fairer or darker—this is determined by their genes at the moment of conception. After birth, health and environmental issues can temporarily change your little one's skin tone. But as soon as these issues are resolved, their skin color will revert to the tone they were born with.

.

6. IS IT SAFE TO GO OUT IN THE SUN?

I think you should start to tally how many times hormones are mentioned in this book since it's again to blame for something you can or cannot do. In this instance, going out in the sun. The changes to your hormones during pregnancy increases the production of melanin in the skin. This excess of skin pigment often results in what is called "the mask of pregnancy," or melasma, where darker patches will appear on the skin (Handel, Miot, & Miot, 2014).

But that's not all; there's a possibility that the surge of pregnancy hormones can make your skin more prone to UV damage, and, thus, increases your risk of skin cancer.

Okay, I'm still not done. Being out in the sun too long can cause overheating and dehydration—both undesirable states to be in when you're pregnant. One study shows a link between high temperatures and babies' birth weight (Cho, 2020). Mommy's who spend too much time in the sun can give birth to a baby at a lower birth weight than desired. This is because the woman's blood vessels need to contract to cool down her body and this causes their baby to lose out on some nutrients.

The experts recommend five to ten minutes of sun exposure two to three times a week (Skin Vision, n.d.)

7. DOES ACTUAL WATER COME OUT WHEN MY WATER BREAKS?

You've seen it in the movies: 'water' floods the expectant mother's feet as they go into labor. Don't worry, it's not always so dramatic in real life—most moms only experience a slow trickle. And no, soon-to-be mommy, it's not water. Your baby is surrounded by amniotic fluid in the amniotic sac meant to protect them. This fluid also helps your little one's lungs and digestive system develop, and works as central heating in your baby's temporary home. Later on in your pregnancy, the fluid in this sac will be mostly made up of your baby's urine plus some nutrients, hormones, and antibodies—it's this liquid that will come out when your water breaks.

8. MY STOMACH IS SORE, AM I IN LABOR?

Every pain, cramp, or sting you feel during pregnancy can be anxiety-inducing. But, even though it leaves you in a panic, there's usually nothing to worry about—it's a common part of pregnancy.

During the first 12 weeks, stomach pain or cramps are, more often than not, caused by your baby bump getting bigger—inside and out. Hormones, constipation, or trapped gas may also be the cause of your discomfort. If the pain goes away after a poo, change of position, or having a nap, then you're in the clear. However, if it continues and gets worse, it's best to seek your doctor's help.

9. WILL EATING GHEE MAKE DELIVERING MY BABY FASTER?

There sure are a lot of old-wives' tales about pregnancy and giving birth. When it comes to ghee's effect on delivery, I'm afraid to say the evidence is anecdotal. The popular belief is that ghee lubricates the vagina, which means your baby will "slide out" effortlessly during normal delivery. There's, unfortunately, no scientific proof to back up this age-old claim.

10. THERE ARE TWO DROPS OF BLOOD IN MY UNDERWEAR. DID I HAVE A MISCARRIAGE?

If there's something even more terrifying than unexpected stomach pain during pregnancy, then it's seeing blood on your undies. But, take a breath—it's not always a sign that something is wrong. A lot of pregnant women will experience spotting. The trick is to distinguish between spotting and heavy bleeding. If you see a trace amount of blood that is lighter than the color of menstrual blood, then you're spotting. In other words, the amount of blood should not be enough to cover a panty liner. When you do need to use a tampon or pad, then it is a medical emergency.

11. CAN I DIET WHEN PREGNANT?

No, no, no! This is the time to eat healthily and more importantly—enough–for you and your growing baby. Mommy, you have a lot to worry about while you're pregnant, the last thing you want to do is add your weight to that list too. There will be more than enough time for you to get your pre-pregnancy body back after you've given birth. For now, avoid any restrictive diets, and focus on eating enough calories to keep you energized and your baby growing. Your body is working hard to support that little human in your tummy, avoid doing anything that will leave it low on important vitamins and minerals.

12. CAN I STILL USE MY FAVORITE SHAMPOO?

Quickly go grab your favorite bottle of shampoo; bring the conditioner too! Let's run through the ingredient list together.

Are any of the following listed?

- Sodium lauryl sulfate
- Parabens
- Methylisothiazolinone (MIT)

- Synthetic fragrances

Chances are, your shampoo contains one or more of these ingredients. But what's the big deal? You only have it on your hair for half a minute, right? Well, your hair follicles are easy entry points into your skin and, thus, your body.

Sodium lauryl sulfate (not to be confused with sodium laureth sulfate, which is safe for use), has been associated with birth defects in animal studies (Journal of the American College of Toxicology, 1983). Out of the other ingredients to watch out for, synthetic fragrances may contain phthalates, which can play havoc on your hormones, and MIT impedes the growth of nerve cells in rats.

Although we don't technically know how these chemicals will affect human fetuses (scientists tend to frown on testing chemicals on pregnant women), it's better to be safe than sorry. This doesn't mean you won't be able to wash your hair for the next nine months! You may just have to change your shampoo to a baby-friendly variety, or if you're too in love with your current shampoo to leave it behind, shampoo less often.

13. SHOULD I DISABLE MY CAR'S AIRBAGS DURING PREGNANCY?

Don't even think about it. Research shows that there's no higher risk of placental separation, fetal distress, or the need for a cesarean section if airbags are deployed during an accident (Ma et al., 2012).

I know your body is different and you think some things may not work the same with that baby bump in the way. But rest assured that you're much safer with a functional airbag than without—it will cushion your belly from impact should you be in an accident.

14. IS IT OKAY TO GO FOR A PIERCING?

The simple answer is yes, but that doesn't make it the safest answer. The chances of any major complications due to getting a piercing are slight but not impossible. There is a possibility that you can develop a serious infection, which will put you and your baby at risk. I suggest you wait until after your baby is born. I mean, do you really need to experience any additional pain and discomfort at the moment?

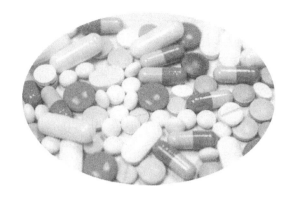

15. MY HEAD HURTS. IS IT OKAY IF I TAKE PAINKILLERS?

It sure is, but not just any painkillers—paracetamol. It has been prescribed by doctors routinely during all stages of pregnancy. Research has given this drug the all-clear (well, almost) when it comes to the safety of your baby. Studies have shown that it poses no particular danger to your unborn baby (Prescrire International, 2012). But as with any medicine taken while pregnant, you want to use it at its lowest effective dose and for the shortest possible amount of time.

16. WHY CAN'T I ENJOY SUSHI WHILE PREGNANT?

The two main reasons are the high mercury levels found in fish and the bacteria and parasites found in uncooked food. Soon-to-be mommies are extra susceptible to infection due to the changes to their immune system when pregnant. Infection increases your risk of miscarriage, preterm delivery, and still-birth, among other things.

What's more, the high mercury content has toxic effects on your baby's nervous system during development and this can result in neurological issues.

17. WILL SPICY FOODS UPSET MY BABY?

I have some good news for all the buffalo hot wings fans out there: eating spicy food during pregnancy can't hurt your little one. That being said, your spicy habit can change the taste of your amniotic fluid (Spahn et al., 2019). But this isn't a bad thing! You may just be breeding the next generation of hot-and-spicy food lovers!

18. IS IT TRUE THAT I SHOULDN'T EAT CHOCOLATE MOUSSE?

Unfortunately, traditional chocolate mousse, tiramisu, uncooked meringues, and other desserts that contain raw egg are off the menu. The reason behind this ban is much the same as that for sushi— you don't want to put yourself and your baby at risk of infection or disease. Since there's a high chance of salmonella in uncooked eggs, it's best to avoid it.

19. ARE ARTIFICIAL SWEETENERS SAFE?

This is one of those answers that's a bit of a mixed bag. While artificial sweeteners are considered safe for pregnant women when used in moderation, there is a possibility that it may increase your little one's risk of obesity later on (Archibald, Dolinsky & Azad, 2018). Although the Food and Drug Administration considers most sweeteners as safe for pregnant women, I want you to keep an eye out for two specific ones: aspartame and saccharin.

You should steer clear of aspartame if you have a rare genetic disease called phenylketonuria (PKU) on your medical chart. Your doctor will also recommend you avoid this artificial sweetener if it shows you have high levels of phenylalanine in your blood.

Then there is saccharin, which although considered safe, can increase your child's risk of bladder tumors when exposed to it in utero (Jensen & Kamby, 1982). In fact, some countries have banned saccharin wholly due to its negative health effects.

20. CAN I STILL USE THE MICROWAVE?

You don't have to worry about your microwave posing a risk to you or your baby. These kitchen appliances rarely leak radiation, and if they do, it is in such small amounts, it's nearly undetectable.

If you're still worried, just stand a few feet away from the microwave when you're using it.

21. SHOULD I AVOID WEARING MAKE-UP WHILE PREGNANT?

The answer is similar to that of question 12 about shampoo, but considering that you use quite a few products to do your makeup, the chemicals you should look out for triples. Even products that are labeled 'natural' or 'organic' may contain questionable ingredients. So, although you don't have to stop wearing make-up, you'll have to become an ingredient detective while you're pregnant.

Here are the ingredients to avoid.

Parabens (propylparaben, butylparaben, isopropylparaben, and methylparaben) have been associated with various development issues in babies.

Retinol is a form of vitamin A usually found in anti-aging products. It goes by other names like retinyl acetate, retinoic, and tretinoin. Consuming too much vitamin A can lead to early-term miscarriage as well as fetal malformation. It's best to avoid this ingredient completely.

Fragrance sounds innocent enough but some companies group hazardous substances under this term. I mentioned phthalates earlier on, but there's also octoxynol, citral, eugenol, coumarin, and geraniol to look out for.

Aluminum powder may give your eyes a shimmery look, but is it really worth it considering that it can be absorbed by the skin causing neurotoxicity and respiratory issues? You can look just as pretty with matte eye shadows.

Talc is generally harmless on its own, but the problem comes in with the small amounts of asbestos present in make-up products. Asbestos is a known carcinogen.

Toluene is a toxic chemical often used in nail polish and hair dye. Although not strictly make-up, I'm sure it is part of your grooming routine, so keep an eye out for it.

22. CAN I PICK UP AND CARRY MY TODDLER WHILE PREGNANT?

Of course you can! There's no reason why your tiny tot needs to miss out on some mommy love while you're carrying baby number two. It's all in how you do it, however—lift with your legs, not your back. You'll also find that sitting them on your hip or below your baby bump will be most comfortable. If you see any sign of spotting or experience pain, then it's a sign that you've overexerted yourself. It doesn't mean something bad will happen, it just means you should pick your child up in a different position and carry them for a shorter time.

That being said, women who have a history of preterm labor or have been diagnosed with a short cervix should avoid picking up anything heavy, including their toddler.

23. IS IT OKAY IF I GO FOR A TEETH-WHITENING PROCEDURE?

There's not a lot of research around this topic—for or against. If you ask your doctor, they will most probably advise you to wait until after delivering and breastfeeding your little one before going for a teeth-whitening procedure. If you consider the adverse effects certain chemicals in shampoo and make-up have on you during pregnancy, then it makes sense to wait before bleaching your teeth.

24. AM I ALLOWED TO DONATE BLOOD?

Close to 52% of pregnant women across the globe have an iron deficiency (Abu-Ouf & Jan, 2015). Considering that your body has a higher demand for iron during pregnancy, you don't want to mess with your iron levels at all. Donating blood will increase your risk of getting iron-deficiency anemia. The general consensus is that women wait six weeks after giving birth before donating blood (American Red Cross, n.d.). On the other hand, the World Health Organization suggests mothers not donate blood for up to nine months after giving birth or three months after their babies are weaned from breast-feeding (World Health Organization, n.d.).

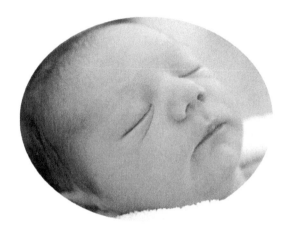

25. DID I HURT MY BABY WHEN I HAD A SMALL FALL?

Remember the amniotic sac I mentioned earlier? It will protect your baby from any bumps and bruises. For you to hurt your baby in a fall, particularly in the first trimester, you'd have to be severely injured yourself. It's only in the third trimester when you should worry after a fall. If you do happen to take a tumble

—anytime during your pregnancy—take precautions. Get in contact with your doctor and find out if they think you should come in for a check-up. They'll probably tell you to look out for bleeding and to count your baby's movements before worrying too much.

26. WHY CAN'T I SLEEP ON MY BACK?

In your first trimester, the position you sleep in doesn't matter that much. However, during the second and third trimesters, the weight of your baby is much heavier than before. Should you then sleep on your back, the weight of your growing uterus and your little one rests on your back, intestines, and the main vein (vena cava) that carries blood to the lower body.

You can imagine how this extra pressure can make your already aching back worse. It can also interfere with your digestion, cause low blood pressure, and restrict circulation, which means your baby gets less oxygen and nutrients.

That doesn't mean you should panic when you wake up and find yourself on your back. As long as you don't sleep in that position for long periods of time, you and your baby will be fine.

27. IS IT OKAY IF I GO FOR A MASSAGE?

Your body and mind go through a lot of stress when you're pregnant, no wonder going for a massage is on your mind. Luckily, massages are considered okay during pregnancy. You may not feel very confident after reading, they're 'okay' and not wonderful, great, or recommended. Well, that is because not all massage techniques are considered safe to do on a pregnant woman—some trigger points in the body may cause premature labor.

If you do decide to go for a massage to improve relaxation, improve your sleep, and leave you with an overall sense of wellness, then find someone who specializes in prenatal massage. Therapists who have been certified to do prenatal massage have received extensive education in techniques that are safe for mommy and baby.

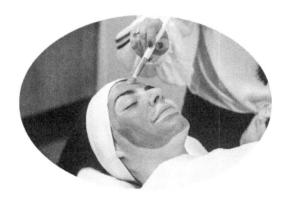

28. CAN I GET A FACIAL WHILE PREGNANT?

You're more than welcome to treat yourself to a basic facial when you're pregnant. I suggest you tell the beauty therapist that you're pregnant beforehand. They'll then select products for sensitive skin instead of for general use since pregnant women's skin is more delicate. Furthermore, they'll know not to use any devices on you during the facial that may be harmful to your baby. Also, discuss with them the ingredients in the products to determine if they're safe to use.

29. CAN I USE SLEEPING PILLS TO HELP ME GET A GOOD NIGHT'S REST?

When it comes to medication, even over-the-counter ones, herbs, and supplements, it is best to avoid taking any during your pregnancy. There are, however, times when you really can't help it. In these cases, you need to talk to your doctor and get their advice. There are a few options they may recommend.

Melatonin is a hormone that the body creates to regulate a person's sleep-wake cycle, so it may seem like the perfect insomnia fix. But since melatonin is classified as a dietary supplement in America, it isn't regulated by the FDA the way other drugs are. This means the impact it has on women and their unborn babies hasn't been well studied. That being said, your doctor may recommend the occasional use of melatonin and at a very small dosage.

If your doctor recommended you take a magnesium supplement to fight off those horrible leg cramps or to combat constipation, then take it at night. Magnesium is a natural muscle relaxant, which may help you sleep.

Your last option should be over-the-counter and prescription sleep aids. Then again, when your insomnia is severe, you may need something stronger than melatonin or magnesium. If this is the case, don't self-medicate—go see your doctor and let them prescribe something to help you sleep.

30. IS BOTOX SAFE DURING PREGNANCY?

No evidence suggests that Botox is unsafe during pregnancy—but nothing points to it being harmless either. Since it is a toxin, it may not be the most sensible decision to inject it into you while you're growing a baby inside of you.

31. CAN I CONTINUE MY ACNE TREATMENT WHILE PREGNANT?

As I mentioned earlier, scientists don't like to give expecting women medication. This means there are no studies to tell us what will happen when a pregnant woman takes X, Y, or Z. The research we do have come from animal studies and where women have continued to use acne treatment of their own volition. From these various studies, researchers could discern between acne medications.

Adapalene: Experts recommend stopping this treatment while pregnant.

Topical antibiotics: Clindamycin is thought to be safe, but it is best to double-check with your doctor or dermatologist.

Oral antibiotics: Cefadroxil can help clear severe acne and hasn't been linked to any birth defects. Other antibiotics often prescribed for the treatment of acne include azithromycin and clarithromycin—both also deemed safe during pregnancy.

Azelaic acid: No birth defects were seen in animal studies.

Benzoyl peroxide: Experts say it is safe to use in limited amounts. I suggest you have a chat with your doctor or dermatologist before you use it during pregnancy.

Dapsone: This is a new-generation acne treatment and thus information on its effects on pregnant women is limited even more. Although no birth defects were noted in animal studies, experts recommend extreme caution when doctors prescribe dapsone to soon-to-be mommies.

Tretinoin: Stop this treatment during pregnancy.

32. IS IT SAFE TO SWIM IN A CHLORINE POOL?

Not only is it safe, but it is also recommended! Taking a dip is a wonderful way to exercise when you're pregnant.

33. IT IS OKAY IF I PUT A HOT PAD ON MY TUMMY?

You can feel free to use a heating pad anywhere on your body, except your abdomen. Heating pads work great to relieve pain in your joints, hips, and back during pregnancy, but you don't want to turn your baby's home into a sauna by placing it on your tummy.

34. IS HOMEOPATHY SAFE WHILE I'M CARRYING A BABY INSIDE ME?

No real side effects of homeopathic medicines on pregnant women have been reported, but you should still stay away from such products while you're pregnant. There is too little scientific data to give homeopathic medicine a yay or a nay, so it is best to avoid it completely. When it comes to your baby, the saying "better safe than sorry" applies a thousand times over.

35. AM I ALLOWED TO EAT HONEY?

Tea with honey; honey on toast—I'm not going to ask you to give up this sweet delight now or while you're breastfeeding. It's true that your little one isn't allowed to eat honey until their one-year-old, but you're not as unlucky.

Honey doesn't affect mommies negatively because their GI system can handle the toxin. An adult's gut is more likely to have enough protective flora in their gut that will keep the Clostridium spores at bay. Also, when your gut is filled with more of the good stuff, there isn't much space for the baddies to grow. A healthy gut is a botulism-free gut. And even though a woman's immune system may be weakened during pregnancy, the digestive flora stays the same, so there's no need to ban honey from your kitchen —just yet.

Then there's the fact that the botulinum toxin cannot be passed to the baby—its molecular weight is too high. So, even if you eat honey and have botulism spores in your own body, they can't pass through the placenta to get to your baby.

36. IS IT OKAY IF I CHANGE MY CAT'S LITTER BOX?

You can change the litter box, yes, but it is better to ask someone else to do it instead. There's a possibility of contracting toxoplasmosis, a parasitic infection found in cat poop. More than 40 million people in America carry the toxoplasma parasite, but not all of them show any symptoms (Centers for Disease Control and Prevention, n.d.). A healthy adult's immune system is capable of keeping the parasite at bay, but the CDC warns that women who are infected with toxoplasma just before falling pregnant or during pregnancy should be aware of severe consequences. If your baby catches toxoplasmosis in the early stages of growth, they may suffer serious birth defects.

37. CAN I CONTINUE TO LOOK AFTER MY PLANTS IN THE GARDEN?

Gardening is a wonderful stress-buster. Furthermore, it's a form of gentle exercise that will help you keep healthy. But that doesn't mean it is entirely risk-free —you must take appropriate measures to protect yourself and your little one from associated hazards.

So, before you get your hands dirty, let's look at the two main risks involved in gardening when you're pregnant.

Toxoplasmosis: You read all about this parasite in the previous answer—but it's not just limited to litter boxes. If you have a cat or a neighboring cat who likes to use your garden as a toilet, then you're at risk of getting in contact with the toxoplasma parasite. Wear gloves, don't touch your face, and wash your hands thoroughly after you've tended your plants.

Chemicals: Pesticides are unsafe even when you're not pregnant. Exposure to herbicides and insecticides may affect your baby's brain and nervous system development.

When you do decide to venture out into the garden, do so at a suitable time. Gardening at noon may lead to sunburn and heatstroke. If you can't avoid gardening during this time, be sure to apply a good sunscreen and wear a sunhat to protect you from the heat. Loose clothing will also keep you cool and comfortable. I recommend you wear long sleeves and pants to make sure you don't come into contact with any contaminated soil or chemicals. Staying hydrated is also vital, so remember to drink water frequently throughout the day.

38. WILL EATING LEFTOVER FOOD HARM MY BABY?

Fresh is best unless home-cooked leftovers were refrigerated properly at 41 degrees Fahrenheit or less. Since you don't know how much time take-away food spends in warming ovens or displays, it's best to steer clear of reheating and eating it later on.

39. CAN I SIT BY A FIRE?

Depending on who you ask, a lot of things you want to do/eat/drink are off-limits. It gets so confusing after a while it may feel like you should just stop living until after you've given birth. That doesn't sound like an enjoyable experience, and, although pregnancy is not all fun and games, there's no need for you to suffer needlessly. That's my long way of saying, whip up a batch of s'mores, and enjoy them next to the fire! As long as there's proper ventilation, there's little risk of smoke from wood fire hurting your baby. Of course, sticking your face into the fire and inhaling the smoke won't be healthy—whether you're pregnant or not.

40. IS IT SAFE TO TAKE MEDICINE TO STOP A RUNNY TUMMY?

There is some anti-diarrheal medicine that is fine to take during pregnancy but you should avoid those that contain bismuth subsalicylate or atropine/diphenoxylate. Your doctor will likely recommend a kaolin-and-pectin type anti-diarrheal.

If you do have a runny tummy, remember to stay hydrated—a lot of fluid is flushing down the toilet so you have to compensate by drinking more. I highly recommend electrolyte-based rehydrating drinks and water as your main sources of fluid intake when you have diarrhea. Fruit juice can make your tummy run even more, and tea, coffee, and sugary drinks will dehydrate you even more.

41. CAN I CALL AN EXTERMINATOR?

During your pregnancy, you want to minimize your contact with chemicals that can be hazardous to you and your baby. Pesticides are poisonous after all! Human studies have shown that exposure to these chemicals increases your child's risk of brain tumors (Greenop et al., 2013). Early experimental evidence suggests that one out of every 250 embryos that have been exposed to active ingredients in pesticides will have a malformation of the forebrain (Addissie et al., 2020). Researchers believe that exposure shortly before conception and during early pregnancy is the most critical window of exposure.

But don't worry mommy, you don't have to let pests pest you—there are alternatives you can use. That's the only reason you're allowed to call an exterminator: to get advice on pregnancy-safe options.

42. AM I ALLOWED TO USE A BODY SCRUB, BUBBLE BATH, SHOWER GEL, AND LOTION?

After reading the previous answers to questions about cosmetics, you should know the answer by now. That being said, there are some body products you'd want to avoid not because of the chemicals used but because they can irritate your skin. Scrubs and exfoliants, for example, can cause micro-tears as your skin is extra-sensitive during pregnancy. This, in turn, can make it easier for those nasty chemicals to get into your body.

You also want to keep a specific eye out for products containing rosemary as this can be particularly aggravating on your skin.

Oh, and lastly, aloe vera. Studies have shown that when taken orally, it may pose a risk to your unborn baby's health. I know you don't plan on eating your body lotion or shower gel (even if you have a strange craving for it), but since your skin absorbs what you put on it, you may want to use it on small areas only.

43. IS IT SAFE TO GO TO MY KICKBOXING CLASS?

Staying active during pregnancy is never a bad idea —it keeps your body and mind healthy, is super good for your baby, and it may even make labor easier. However, kickboxing isn't really the type of exercise you should be doing right now. Getting kicked in the stomach right now is a risk you don't want to take. There's also the danger of you falling since your balance in the second half of pregnancy isn't quite what it should be.

But just because you can't be a karate mom doesn't mean you can't walk, swim, cycle, or do something else that isn't a contact activity. If you've enjoyed going for a morning run before your pregnancy, you can still continue to do so as long as you sip on water throughout to stay hydrated and do it at a time of day when it's not too hot.

44. WILL WEARING HEELS HURT MY UNBORN BABY?

Some ladies find it extremely difficult to trade in their nine-inch heels for a pair of pumps or worse, sneakers. I get it, but it may be best for you and your baby's well-being to put your fashion sense on hold during pregnancy. I know some women have worn heels while pregnant and came out unscathed at the other end—and so did their little ones. But it's just not worth the risk. In fact, there are many reasons why giving up heels during pregnancy is the best thing to do—not only will they be uncomfortable to wear, they can be hazardous. Slipping, falling, and hurting your baby is only one of the dangers.

45. CAN I EAT PEANUT BUTTER?

You definitely can. Peanuts and peanut butter contain polyunsaturated fat and antioxidants. They're also rich in folate, a B vitamin that can decrease your baby's risk of any neural tube defects. Of course, if you're allergic, then peanut butter and any products that contain peanuts are big no-nos.

46. IS IT OKAY IF I GO HORSE RIDING?

As you probably figured out by now, any activities that can lead to a fall or abdominal trauma are advised against. However, if you want to hop onto a horse during your first trimester, you're more than welcome to. That is if you have experience riding a horse and plan on going for a walk and not a gallop, then your baby should be fine. That's because your baby is inside your pelvic girdle—a bony structure that will protect them should you fall. As the pregnancy progresses, your baby moves higher up in the abdomen and loses this protection.

Furthermore, the bumping motion may cause your placenta to separate from the uterus—known as placental abruption.

47. WHAT'S THE VERDICT ON ANTIBIOTICS WHILE PREGNANT?

Doctors still prescribe antibiotics to pregnant women, but they choose the specific medication carefully and with the safety of you and your baby in mind. They will consider the type of antibiotic, how long you've been pregnant, how much to take, and for how long, and what side effects it may have on your pregnancy.

Here's a list of antibiotics generally prescribed by doctors since they're considered safe for pregnant women.

- Penicillins
- Cephalosporins
- Erythromycin
- Clindamycin

48. SHOULD I STOP WEARING SUNSCREEN?

There are more opinions on what you should and shouldn't do during pregnancy than there are babies born a day–385,000 by the way. A lot of the time, the views and outlooks don't even match. But one thing is certain, dermatologists agree that you shouldn't stop protecting yourself from harmful UV rays when you're pregnant. It's actually the perfect time to reaffirm your commitment to healthy skin.

Apart from the obvious reasons to wear sunscreen—chiefly skin cancer—your skin is more sensitive when you're pregnant, as you know. This opens you up to a lot of pregnancy-related conditions like hyperpigmentation, which can cause blotches, patches, and dots of varying colors on your skin.

To choose the best sunscreen, here are some things to keep in mind.

Look for broad-spectrum sunscreen—they offer protection against UVA and UVB rays. It also has to have a sun protection factor (SPF) of 30 or higher.

Mineral or physical sunscreens are also better options for pregnant women. They're hypoallergenic and don't get absorbed by the skin. Choose a sunscreen that is labeled water-resistant or has zinc oxide and/or titanium dioxide listed as active ingredients

Of course, the best sun protection you can get is staying out of the sun altogether. If you do go out, try to stay in shady sections between 10 am and 2 pm when the sun is at its strongest.

49. IS IT SAFER TO SMOKE LIGHTER CIGARETTES WHILE PREGNANT?

It's a known fact that lighting up during pregnancy increases your risk of spontaneous miscarriage, preterm delivery, low birth weight, placental abruption, stillbirth, etc. (Eskenazi, Prehn & Christiansen, 1995). Smoking a 'light' cigarette does not remove these and other risks, but can, in fact, be more harmful (Elton-Marshall et al., 2010). Cigarette companies in some countries aren't even allowed to label their products as 'light' or 'low-tar' anymore.

50. CAN I GET INTO A JACUZZI?

Remember how overheating and dehydration should be avoided when you're pregnant. Well, if you've ever been in a jacuzzi, you know that it's not really possible to avoid either of those two. There's also the added risk of fainting when you get out of a sauna, jacuzzi, hot tub, or steam room during pregnancy.

But why exactly do you overheat and dehydrate? It all comes down to your body's inability to lose heat effectively in such warm and wet conditions, which raises your body's core temperature. When this happens, more blood floods to your skin to help your body cool down—taking away blood flow from internal organs, such as your brain. This can make you feel faint. Add to that the fact that the hormonal changes in your body may make you feel dizzy even on the best of days, and you're asking for trouble.

51. IS ACUPUNCTURE SAFE WHILE PREGNANT?

A lot of soon-to-be mommies turn to alternative medicine when pregnant because they believe it is healthier. Although this is true in many instances, you still have to do your research when you're considering any type of alternative treatment. Acupuncture is considered safe but it does have a few risks. Most of the negative effects of acupuncture are mild, such as general soreness, redness, mild infection where the needles were inserted, and injury if the needles were placed too deeply. That's a small price to pay for the many advantages that you'll get from going for this treatment. That being said, you have to make sure you go to a trained professional. There are acupuncture and acupressure points that can hurt you and your baby. Take the pressure points in the ankle, for example, they are said to induce contractions—the last thing you want in early pregnancy. However, if you're getting impatient and you're past your due date, you can give it a try to help hurry your baby up.

52. IS IT DANGEROUS TO BE AROUND SMOKERS?

In question 49, we looked at the dangers of smoking during pregnancy. I am sorry to tell you that being surrounded by smoke while you're pregnant isn't any healthier. In fact, pregnant women who are exposed to secondhand smoke are more likely to bring a baby into this world who has a low birth weight and we know that these little ones start life off with a disadvantage (U.S. Department of Health and Human Services, 2010).

Also, babies born to mothers who smoked or were exposed to secondhand smoke after birth have a higher chance of dying from sudden infant death syndrome (SIDS) than babies who live in a smoke-free environment (U.S. Department of Health and Human Services, 2006). Another negative consequence of being around smokers is that your baby will have weaker lungs and this increases their risk for various health conditions.

53. IS IT OKAY IF I COLOR MY HAIR DURING PREGNANCY?

Swollen ankles, puffy face, stretch marks...do you really have to deal with roots and grays while you're pregnant too? Thank goodness, no! Although hair dye should be approached with the same caution you would other cosmetic products at this time, there's no reason to let your hair bring you down. As long as you take certain precautions, no harm will come to your baby. You already know which ingredients to avoid, but there are a few tips to keep things as safe as possible for your baby-to-be.

Wait until the second trimester. I know this may be a hard ask, considering that those pesky pregnancy hormones have probably caused your hair to grow faster than usual. Wait, that isn't a bad thing, is it? So hormones aren't all bad, after all! Anyway, although research on this matter is sparse, experts agree that your baby has a lot of growing to do during the first 12 weeks, so adding chemicals to the mix may not be a good idea. Yes, there's not really any hard evidence that your body absorbs enough chemicals to be harmful to your baby, but it's one of those "why take the chance?" scenarios.

Select the safest techniques. I know those roots are bugging you, but root touch-ups and root-to-tip color changes require the dye to be applied directly to the scalp, making it easier for your body to soak up the chemicals. Ask your hairdresser for a safer alternative where the color is painted directly on the hair, for example pulling the hair through a cap and then applying the dye.

Choose a gentle color. The type of dye you use also plays an important role. Those with an ammonia-free base or maybe a semi-permanent option is best at this time. Henna or vegetable dyes are also less-toxic but check the label anyway before you commit to it— some products that claim to be 'natural' often contain just as many chemicals as their counterparts.

54. CAN I GO SEE A CHIROPRACTOR?

I don't know what I would've done without my chiropractor. When you're pregnant, your body produces more ligament and joint-loosening hormones to make it easier for baby to greet the world. Although you'll be happy these hormones were released when it's time to give birth to your little one, you're not going to be too impressed during pregnancy. Your loose joints and ligaments in combination with your baby bump rapidly lower your center of gravity. This leaves your body in a "loosey-goosey" state, which will do quite a number on your spine.

This is where chiropractic care is invaluable—these "out-of-whack-back crackers" as they're affectionately known will realign your spinal cord and everything that surrounds it. You will also come across claims that these adjustments can control morning sickness, reduce the likelihood of miscarriage, and lower your risk of giving birth to a preemie. Moreover, the realignment may relax the ligaments and muscles in your pelvis, which helps breech babies turn themselves. Read up on the Webster Technique if you're interested in this chiropractic method.

Of course, you can't just go to any chiropractor. You have to do your research and find one trained to work with soon-to-be mommies. They should have a special table where there won't be any pressure on your belly, and they won't ask you to lie flat on your back either. I also suggest you check with your OB-GYN first—there may be a reason you don't know about why spinal realignment may not be the best thing for you and your baby.

55. IS IT SAFE TO GO TO PILATES CLASS?

This is another good form of workout for pregnant women—it's a non-impact exercise that increases flexibility, strength, and muscle tone. Pilates also has a strong focus on the core, which means it can improve your posture, help ease backaches, and even aid with labor and delivery.

56. AM I ALLOWED TO FLY?

It's safe to fly if there aren't any complications your doctor mentioned. However, when you reach the 37-week mark, most airlines will not allow you to fly. In general, air travel before week 36 of pregnancy is believed to be safe, but make sure to double check with your doctor just in case. They may caution against air travel if you're experiencing any complications that may require emergency care or be worsened by air travel. You also have to consider the duration of the flight.

57. IS DOING YOGA DANGEROUS?

Prenatal yoga can be considered a childbirth-preparation exercise. It is multifaceted and encourages stretching, focused breathing, and mental grounding —the last two being especially beneficial in lowering your stress levels during pregnancy.

To all the yoga mommies out there, or if you plan on taking up yoga as one of your exercises while you're pregnant, you will have to modify some poses. I recommend you go to a yoga class that specifically tailors to pregnant women.

58. CAN I CONTINUE TO DRINK MY MORNING CUPPA?

Is it possible for anyone to even have a personality without first drinking a cup of coffee in the morning?

I doubt it! Luckily you won't need to give up your morning coffee while you're pregnant. Experts say that one 12-ounce cup of coffee or 200 milligrams of caffeine a day is safe for you and your growing baby (American College of Obstetricians and Gynecologist, n.d.).

I know that isn't nearly enough for the hardcore caffeine addicts out there but any more than the recommended 200 mg and you increase your risk of miscarriage—although the existing evidence is inconclusive. Caffeine does, however, permeate the placental barrier, so I recommend you stick to what doctors say, just to be safe.

If coffee isn't your energy boost of choice, eight ounces of brewed tea contains 48 mg of caffeine and you'll be getting a 100 mg caffeine kick if you drink 8 ounces of an energy drink.

Keep in mind that the chocolate you nibble on during the day also contains caffeine and so does a lot of sodas.

59. I LIKE MY STEAK RARE. IS IT OKAY TO EAT IT THIS WAY WHILE PREGNANT?

Although pink and red may be your favorite colors because you're having a girl, that's the last thing you want to see when it comes to your meat. Undercooked meat and poultry are known to harbor bacteria such as e. coli, salmonella, trichinella, and toxoplasma.

The bottom line is if the meat you ordered comes out a little too pink—send it back. Your baby's safety is in your hands, now isn't the time to be bashful.

60. IS IT SAFE TO EAT JERKY?

Nope! Although jerky isn't raw meat in the traditional sense, it's not cooked in a way that kills bacteria. Jerky is dried meat and you can't be sure of the temperature it was dried at. So, for all the reasons why you can't eat bloody meat, you can't eat jerky.

But there's more; jerky is high in salt and may cause your blood pressure to spike. This increases your risk of preterm labor and preeclampsia.

61. IS IT OKAY TO GO TO A LIVE MUSIC CONCERT?

There's nothing like a night out on town to blow some steam off and feel human again. When it comes to live music concerts, you're probably worried about the booming bass and loud vocals harming your baby. Well, the good news is that the music isn't loud enough and the exposure isn't long enough to cause any damage.

Here are some interesting facts about your baby's hearing development:

- They only begin to detect partial noises at the 16-week mark of pregnancy.
- At 24 weeks, their outer, middle, and inner ear are well-developed. Your baby will start to turn their head in response to familiar voices and sounds.

But that still doesn't mean they'll be able to hear the pumping beats at a concert. The amniotic fluid and your body create a sound barrier that muffles any sounds. Furthermore, your baby's eardrum and middle ear can't amplify sounds yet, so sounds that are quite loud to you will be background noise to your baby.

62. I WANT A TATTOO OF MY BABY'S FIRST SONAR. CAN I GET ONE WHILE PREGNANT?

The main reason why getting a tattoo while pregnant isn't a great idea is because it poses the risk of getting an infectious disease like Hepatitis B, C, or HIV. These infections are transmitted by tainted blood that enters the bloodstream. Although most licensed tattoo parlors use sterile needles, you can't be too safe.

There's also the chemicals in the tattoo dye to consider—there's a possibility that they may affect your little one's development in the first 12 weeks of pregnancy (American Pregnancy Association, n.d.). Although there are very few studies on getting tattoos during pregnancy and the effects during each trimester are unknown, doctors advise waiting until after giving birth.

63. CAN I GO BOWLING WITH MY FRIENDS?

Check with your doctor first, as with all physical activities. I know bowling isn't a contact sport or an exercise where you'll overexert yourself, the weight of the ball can put stress on your shoulders, elbow joints, and lower back. It is overall a good idea to cover any safety concerns your doctor may have. And if you do get the green light from your doctor, take the proper precautions.

Here are some safety tips:

- Don't go too heavy. If you have good aim, you'll still get that strike you're hoping for, even when using a lower weight ball.
- Go duckpin bowling. The balls are smaller and easier to handle.
- Don't cross over the line. The lanes are plastered with oils to help the balls down the lane easier. Don't overstep onto a slick spot.
- Listen to your body. If something you're doing doesn't feel good—don't do it. You can sit out a round or two and try a

different technique when it's your turn again.

- Bend your knees. This will relieve strain off of your back and keep your spine aligned.

64. WHY SHOULDN'T I RAISE MY ARMS ABOVE MY HEAD?

Oh dear, if you weren't allowed to raise your arms above your head, you wouldn't be able to do much of anything while growing your baby. Luckily this is just another old wive's tale. Older generations believed that raising your arms over your head while pregnant would cause the baby's umbilical cord to wrap around their neck.

It's strange that they believed this since the umbilical cord isn't connected to your arms in any way but runs between the placenta and the baby's stomach.

When a baby's cord does wrap around their neck, it is because of the twisting and turning they do in the uterus before birth. It happens to about a third of all births.

65. IS IT SAFE TO RIDE A BICYCLE DURING PREGNANCY?

Getting on your bike and going for a ride is a great form of exercise. Wind in your hair, fresh air, quiet—riding a bicycle won't only get your heart going, it will help anxiety melt away. That being said, as soon as your center of gravity shifts (during the third trimester), you may want to think of another exercise. You're going to be very clumsy during that time and you do not want to risk falling and injuring your little one.

66. MY SKIN LOOKS PALE. IS IT OKAY IF I GO FOR A SPRAY TAN?

The active ingredient in spray tan is dihydroxyace-tone (DHA)—a non-toxic substance that can't go beyond the outer layer of skin and thus can't harm your baby. However, absorption through the skin isn't the main concern here, inhaling the spray is. The effects of breathing in DHA are unknown, so using fake tan creams and lotions may be the safer option. Of course, there is a risk that you might have an allergic reaction. Since your skin is ultra-sensitive during pregnancy thanks to the change in hormone levels, you may suddenly have a negative reaction to cosmetics you've used before. I recommend you test the product on a small patch of skin first, just in case.

If you're considering taking tanning pills, don't. They contain large quantities of canthaxanthin or beta-carotene—known food colorings—that can be toxic to your unborn baby.

67. CAN I HELP PAINT MY BABY'S NURSERY WHILE PREGNANT?

It's unlikely that paint fumes will harm your baby—most modern household paints are safe for the most part. There's only a risk if you use solvent-based paints. I also suggest you don't strip any old paint-work while you're pregnant. The paint flakes may contain traces of lead, which is bad for you and your baby.

If you do paint or decorate while pregnant, you can reduce any would-be risks in the following ways:

- Wait until you're 13-weeks-pregnant before you paint or decorate your baby's room. The small risk that there is will be greater during weeks o to 12—the time your little one's organs start to grow.

- Use water-based paint and not solvent-based paints. Spray paint should also be avoided.
- Make sure there is ventilation in the room you're painting.
- Wear protective clothing.
- Don't eat or drink in the room you're painting in.
- Wash your hands after you're done working with the paint and any other decoration materials.

68. IS IT SAFE TO GO ON A SUNBED?

This isn't so much an answer for baby's safety but mommy's. Remember how I've mentioned throughout this book that a pregnant woman's skin is extra sensitive due to hormonal changes? Well, that is exactly why you shouldn't go on a sunbed while expecting. Your skin is more likely to get burned by the ultraviolet rays sunbeds give out.

If nothing can keep you away from getting that tanned glow, then make sure to use a higher factor sun lotion than you normally would. It may take a little longer to get the skin shade you want, but it will lessen the chance of you walking out with blisters and skin damage.

69. CAN I GET A MANICURE AND PEDICURE?

One advantage of the surge of pregnancy hormones is that your nails will grow longer and stronger in the blink of an eye. You're more than welcome to take advantage of this time and treat yourself to a mani or pedi. The chemicals in nail polish can't be absorbed through your nail bed and have never been linked to birth defects. The only thing that might be a problem is if the salon isn't well-ventilated. The fumes are pretty strong and you may get nauseated by them. If that is the case, ask to sit close to a window.

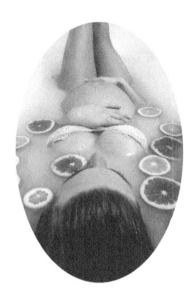

70. IS IT TRUE THAT I SHOULD AVOID SOAKING IN A BATH?

I feel sorry for the old wive's who believed this tale—they missed out on a lot of soothing baths. If you follow a few simple rules, taking a bath may quickly turn into the highlight of your day. Of course, if you were like me, you may find yourself soaking in the tub more than once a day while pregnant. It's great for backache and other pregnancy symptoms like swollen feet.

Before you hop in, make sure your bath water is no hotter than 98.6 degrees F. I used a child's bathtub toy thermometer to ensure the water was and stayed at the perfect temperature. There's no need to rush; get comfortable in the tub and adjust the water as needed (using the thermometer as your guide, of course.)

71. IS LUNCH MEAT SAFE?

Lunch meat or deli meats are cooked meats that are pre-sliced—you can also call it sandwich meat, cold cuts, or sliced meats. Lunchmeat is so popular that most people are surprised when they learn that pregnant women aren't allowed to eat it. But what pregnancy concerns are there when you enjoy some deli meats? Well, you can thank the bacteria listeria monocytogenes for smashing your three-meat sandwich dreams.

Although the infection rate of listeria is on the low side annually (only 2,500 individuals), you must remember that as a pregnant woman, you're more susceptible to it. If your growing baby is exposed to it, the consequences can be devastating. So, although you enjoy a lunch meat sandwich for lunch each day, the safest thing you can do at the moment is to avoid them. Some people may even suggest you cook lunch meat until steaming to remove any traces of listeria, but if at all possible, avoid it altogether. There are other delicious options out there that don't even have a 0.0001% of harming your little one.

72. CAN I STILL ENJOY A SEAFOOD PLATTER WHILE PREGNANT?

Fish and seafood are great for you and your baby—when selected and prepared correctly. There's no need to banish all seafood from the menu while you're pregnant; most fish are perfectly safe to eat as long as you cook them properly and they're not high in mercury.

When you do buy fish, make sure it isn't discolored and doesn't have a foul odor. And when you're playing chef and preparing the catch of the day, follow these guidelines:

Slip the point of a sharp knife into the flesh and pull it aside. If cooked thoroughly, the flesh will be opaque and the lakes will begin to separate.

Let fish cooked in the oven stand for three or four minutes. It will continue cooking while it cools down.

When you're cooking prawns and lobster, they should turn red when cooked with pearly-opaque flesh. Scallops will be firm with a milky-white color. The shells of clams, mussels, and oysters will open when they're done. Those that stay closed after the cooking time has passed should be thrown away.

If you're cooking seafood in the microwave, check several spots to make sure it is cooked throughout.

If you have a food thermometer, make use of it to check that the seafood has reached 145.5 degrees F and you'll know it is ready to eat.

When it comes to the mercury content of fish, you should avoid:

- Shark
- Marlin
- Swordfish
- Catfish
- Orange roughy
- Ray
- Barramundi
- Gemfish
- Ling
- Southern bluefin tuna

73. I LIKE LIFTING HEAVY WEIGHTS. IS IT OKAY IF I DO IT DURING PREGNANCY?

Lifting heavy things is dangerous when you're pregnant. You can hurt your back, twist or pull something, or experience high blood pressure during the exercise. That being said, weight training isn't off-limits. Instead of going heavy, you can use moderate weights for multiple repetitions (reps). There are a lot of benefits to strength training for pregnant women, including building stamina which will help a lot during labor.

Here are some other benefits of lifting weights while pregnant.

- Helps prevent aches and pains and your tummy gets heavier.
- Strengthens your body muscles and whole body for labor.
- Prepares you for picking up, carrying, and pushing around your new little human.

Here are some weight exercises that aren't recommended for pregnant women.

1. Crossfit type training where you're lifting heavy weights in timed intervals.

2. General circuit classes where you have to use barbells and fast movements.

3. Exercises that require you to use heavy barbells behind your neck.

4. Don't do deadlifts, clean and press, and upright rows. The bar may bump your tummy. These exercises also need a lot of control to keep the correct posture—something that is difficult during pregnancy.

5. Weighted sit-ups after 12 weeks.

6. Abdominal rotation exercises.

74. ARE SOFT CHEESES HEALTHY WHILE PREGNANT?

Brie, camembert, chevre, and other mold-ripened soft cheese should be avoided. Blue-veined cheeses like Danish blue or gorgonzola are also best left off of your plate. Since they're made with mold, there's a danger they may contain listeria, and judging by the answer on lunch meats, we know that is not something we want to eat.

75. SHOULD I GET A PAP SMEAR DURING MY PREGNANCY?

Getting a pap smear or pap test early in your pregnancy forms part of routine prenatal care. It takes only a few minutes and the results are sent off to the lab to check for any nasty surprises. If any abnormal cervical cells are picked up, it could indicate the presence of cervical cancer.

After going for a pap smear, you may experience some light spotting. This is because your cervix is sensitive during pregnancy. If you're worried about miscarriage, don't be. The fertilized egg is implanted high up in the uterus and not near the cervix—usually. If that is not the case, the cervix is thick enough in the first trimmest to prevent any disturbance to the implanted fertilized egg.

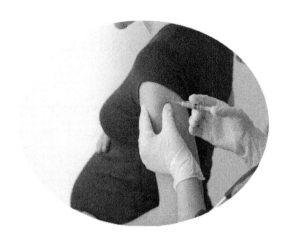

76. ARE VACCINATIONS SAFE DURING THIS TIME?

Some are, yes. Your doctors may even recommend you get two vaccines during your pregnancy.

Flu vaccine

If you get pregnant during the flu season, getting the jab will protect yourself and your baby from flu-related complications—for several months after birth even!

Tdap vaccine

The best time in your pregnancy to get this vaccine is between 27 and 36 weeks. It protects you and your little one from whooping cough (pertussis). If you didn't get it during your pregnancy, it is recommended that you get it immediately after giving birth.

The antibodies your body will make in response to these vaccines won't only protect you, but will also cross the placenta and protect your baby from specific diseases early in life.

77. CAN I RIDE BUMPER CARS WITH MY TODDLER?

Mommy, there will be more than enough time later to enjoy such activities. It's not safe to do it while you're pregnant. Your body is dealing with a lot during pregnancy—you don't want to make things extra hard by adding things that can cause nausea and dizziness. Worse yet, you can hurt your back, neck, and pelvis muscles.

Play it safe and avoid any behaviors that will bounce and jostle your body and your baby all over the place. Yes, these activities are fun, but they're not worth the risk.

78. I WANT TO GO ON A ROLLERCOASTER RIDE. IS THAT OKAY?

Okay, I know I just said to avoid any jostling and bouncing, but if you're an adrenaline junky and you have to get your rollercoaster fix, then make sure to do it during the first trimester. The placenta is still developing at this stage and is less likely to be disturbed by such jarring movement.

But I know most mommies won't do it—the payoff just isn't worth it. I mean, four seconds of—some call it fun, I call it terror—doesn't come close to the love you feel for that little heartbeat inside of you.

79. CAN I CONTINUE TO GET BRAZILIAN WAXES MONTHLY?

With all the unwanted hair growth you'll be experiencing thanks to the pregnancy hormones, you may even decide to start getting Brazilian waxes if you don't already. Luckily you won't be doing anything to harm your baby, but I can't say the same for you. No, I'm not talking about the pain that goes hand-in-hand with waxing. I'm talking about your skin—it may be too sensitive to handle waxing or you may experience an allergic reaction to the product. Apply the wax on a small area before venturing to the more sensitive parts of your body.

If you do find that pregnancy and waxing don't mix, you may want to shave for the time being—or until your baby bump gets in the way at least.

80. IS IT SAFE TO DO MY DAILY HOUSE CLEANING ROUTINE?

Wouldn't it be great if all your daily chores disappeared as soon as you got pregnant? If only dreams came true, but unfortunately we're left to deal with dusty tables, sticky floors, mountains of washing, and yesterday's dishes nevermind the fact that we're growing tiny humans. Since getting pregnant unfortunately doesn't render you incapable of keeping the house clean, here are some rules to follow.

Avoid the fumes: Now may be the time to go green. Not only will natural cleaning products keep you safe during pregnancy, but it will also prepare you for when your little one comes home. Harsh chemicals don't belong in a house where soon-to-be-mommies or babies live. As a start, make a mix of vinegar, baking soda, and lemon—you won't be disappointed.

Stay away from the kitty litter: I already covered this in a previous answer but as a refresher, toxoplasma is found in cat poop and can cause toxoplasmosis, which can cause miscarriage or pre-term birth.

Protect your back: It may not be a problem at first, but your back will start to niggle as your pregnancy moves along—that's a heavy bump to carry around! Furthermore, your center of gravity shifts in month four and if you're not careful when lifting or carrying things, you can seriously hurt your back. So, get into the habit of using proper back mechanics while doing chores.

Take care of your belly: Your belly will get in the way—a lot. Spaces you normally fit in will all of the sudden be too small, you'll struggle to pick up the laundry basket, corners and cabinets will seemingly have moved a few inches; there are a lot of things you'll have to think about and work around as you grow bigger. As you know, it's highly unlikely that you'll hurt your baby if you bump your belly, but you can hurt yourself and that's not nice either. Be kind to yourself.

81. AM I ALLOWED TO INDULGE IN CHOCOLATE?

Everything in moderation as they say. If you plan on eating seven jumbo-sized candy bars, it's not going to be good for you or your baby, but a bite of chocolate every now and again won't do any harm.

82. CAN I USE A HAIR RELAXER?

These products contain a cocktail of harsh chemicals. Although there isn't concrete proof that these chemicals will harm your little one, I suggest you err on the side of caution. Go au naturel while you're pregnant; it can be liberating to let yourself go just a little.

83. CAN MY CAT, DOG, OR TODDLER HURT MY BABY?

If you're worried about your baby bump being in the way when an excited Fido jumps up to greet you, or when your toddler runs slam-bam into your belly to give you a hug, then you can relax. Your body and the amniotic sac and fluid will cushion your baby from any harm. The only time when you'll have to pay extra care is closer to your due date.

When it comes to cats harming your baby, they're not big enough to cause any physical harm but they do carry toxoplasma and I think by now you know that's something to be cautious of.

However, if you've had your cat for a while, the like-lihood is that you've already had toxoplasmosis and are now immune to it. You can go for a blood test to confirm your immunity but only before you conceive —the test can't tell whether you're carrying the anti-bodies from an old infection or dealing with a new infection.

84. HOW DO I GET MY SOCKS ON?

I had a good chuckle at this question—I remember how frustrating it was when I felt increasingly whale-like and had to put on socks. I tried a few times until I stopped trying and wore slip-on shoes or sandals exclusively.

One of my clients used to sit on the edge of the bed spreading her legs as wide apart as possible. She'd then lean down in-between her legs and put one foot's sock on while leaning against the other leg.

Another method is to put a foot over the opposite knee and do it that way. You'll have to find out what works for you—if anything does, that is.

85. IS GOING INTO LABOR REALLY THAT PAINFUL?

You'd be happy to read that it's not as bad for everyone as it's shown to be in the movies. The level of labor pain is different for every woman, and can even vary from pregnancy to pregnancy. Some experience a mild pain that resembles menstrual cramps, while others have exceptionally strong cramps. Usually, it's not the contraction on its own that is the hardest, but the fact that they keep coming combined with the time between them getting less and less.

86. WHY AM I ITCHY?

It's a "pregnancy thing" believe it or not. It's caused by the increase of certain chemicals in the blood. Later on, as your tummy gets bigger, the stretching over that area will cause your skin to feel itchy.

87. WILL MY WATER BREAKING STAIN ANYTHING?

Unless there are traces of blood or placenta in it, it won't. If you're worried about spoiling some expensive sheets, or an antique couch, cover a plastic sheet with a towel and sit or lie on it instead. You can start doing this from 37 weeks and up.

88. IS IT POSSIBLE TO STAY MODEST IN THE HOSPITAL?

Childbirth is anything but modest. A room full of people will help you push a tiny human out of a very small opening. This fact stresses some women out more than anything else. Unfortunately, it's a part of the process you can't change. The only control you really have is whether or not you want to allow nursing students into the delivery room – if you are comfortable with thatyou can discuss it with your doctor.

One thing that may make you relax is to remind yourself that doctors and nurses are used to nudity—they see people naked in all kinds of ways and it doesn't phase them anymore. It's never nice to think of yourself as "just a number" but maybe thinking of yourself as "just another naked patient" may help you feel less shy.

89. WILL I POOP ON THE HOSPITAL BED?

Poop happens, as they say. The muscles you use to go number two are the exact same ones you'll use to push out your baby. So, you won't be the first preg-nant woman to poop in the delivery room, and you won't be the last. It can also happen more than once during the labor process but is most common right before the baby crowns. And you know what? You probably won't even realize that you let something slip—your attention will be elsewhere.

90. CAN I DRIVE MYSELF TO THE HOSPITAL WHILE IN LABOR?

This isn't an ideal scenario, especially if you're a first-time mom. If you haven't gone through labor before, you won't know how it will start and how quickly it will progress. In fact, not even mommies giving birth to their second or third child will know. If you happen to have extremely painful contractions, you may be involved in an accident and be forced to give birth in the street. I recommend you phone your health insurance to find out what it will cost to phone an ambulance just in case no one could drive you. Alternatively, call an Uber? That will be a thrilling story to tell to their other customers!

91. WHY DOES MY BABY HATE ME?

Your baby doesn't hate you. I know it may feels like that, but they actually love you so much that they're willing to let go and cry as much as they need to. A lot of mommies complain that their newborn is a real grumpy grump when around them. Well, you're their safety; you love them more than anything in the world and also provide them with everything they need to survive. And despite how you may perceive their constant crying and fussing, your baby loves and trusts you so much that they feel safe enough to release all stress when they're with you. Your little one will instinctively know that when they're tired, overstimulated, uncomfortable, or overwhelmed, they can let it all out—you'll love them no matter how 'bad' they are.

92. IS MY BABY BUMP NORMAL?

Everyone grows differently. Some women are big, others are small; some carry high, others low, or wide.

It doesn't matter how your tummy looks, if the doctor says everything inside is going as it should, then you're home free. Stop worrying and start enjoying your pregnancy!

93. MY PEE IS GREENISH. SHOULD I BE CONCERNED?

Just when you think pregnancy can't get any weirder, you get green urine. Various things can cause your urine to turn green, chiefly medication. If you notice that your urine is a strange color, give your doctor a ring and find out if you should go see them. They'll be able to tell you if any medications they may have prescribed can cause green urine. For example, promethazine used for allergies and nausea is known to turn urine green.

94. IS MY WEIGHT HEALTHY?

Your doctor is the best person to answer this question since they see you regularly and know what you weigh. But, as a guideline, if you were an average weight before getting pregnant, then you should gain somewhere between 25 and 35 pounds during your pregnancy. Underweight women should pick up 28 to 40 pounds, and overweight women are looking at 15 to 25 pounds.

You should gain two to four pounds in the first three months, followed by one pound a week for the duration of your pregnancy. However, if you're expecting twins, you should gain 35 to 25 pounds—averaging one and a half pounds per week after the initial weight gain in the first three months.

If you've ever wondered where the extra weight goes, here's a basic breakdown:

- Baby: eight pounds
- Placenta: two to three pounds

- Amniotic fluid: two to three pounds
- Breast tissue: two to three pounds
- Blood supply: four pounds
- Stored fat for delivery and breastfeeding: nine pounds
- Uterus: two to five pounds

That gives you a total of between 25 and 35 pounds.

95. AM I DRINKING ENOUGH WATER?

You need to drink more water than the average person when you're pregnant. Your body will need extra fluids to make amniotic fluid, build new tissue, carry nutrients, produce extra blood, flush out toxins, and enhance digestion. To do all this, you need to drink no less than eight glasses of water a day. Another way to check if you're drinking enough water is to look at the color of your urine—if it is pale or colorless, you're on the right track.

96. WHEN SHOULD I GO TO THE HOSPITAL?

Longer, stronger, closer together, means your baby is on the way. If you need more detail: when your contractions are five minutes apart, one minute long, and continues for one hour or longer, it's time to go to the hospital.

Contractions that aren't strong or long yet, may indicate the early phase of labor. It's best to rest and leave your body to do its thing at home until the real contractions begin.

Also, I know contractions are horrible to experience, but take a deep breath and smile—you'll soon be meeting the tiny little human you carried inside you for nine months.

97. WHAT PAIN MEDS CAN I GET WHEN IN LABOR?

There are three types of pain-relief options you'll have when giving birth.

Nitrous oxide: Also known as "laughing gas" may be administered through a face mask or tube in your mouth. It won't take the pain away entirely, but it does take the edge off. Women who choose nitrous oxide usually do so because they have the control.

Pethidine: This pain killer is related to morphine and heroin, so you can expect it to be strong. Doctors usually inject it into a muscle in your bum, but they may also decide to administer it intravenously. It lasts anywhere from two to four hours.

Epidural anesthesia: By far the most effective pain relief during labor. It's not only used for natural births but for cesarean sections too. It allows the mother to stay awake and ready to hold their baby for the first time. It is an anesthetic injected into the lining of the spinal cord and makes you feel numb from the waist down. Epidural injections have more side effects than the other pain-killer meds mentioned but none are life-threatening.

98. HOW MANY PEOPLE CAN COME TO THE BIRTH?

Most hospitals will allow up to three people in the delivery room but it depends on hospital policy.

Phone your hospital to find out how many people can hold your hand during your baby's delivery. Just keep in mind that hospital policy is there for your safety, so if you can't invite your mom, dad, grandma, and high-school bestie into the delivery room with you and your partner, then don't be mad at the hospital.

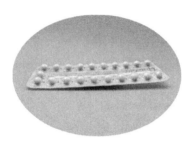

99. CAN I START CONTRACEPTION WHILE PREGNANT?

I'm not sure why you'd want to add more hormones to the cocktail already running through your blood. If you're worried that you'll get pregnant while pregnant, it's very unlikely. It's only in extremely rare cases that a woman can get pregnant when a baby is already growing inside her. When you're pregnant your ovaries take a break and stop releasing eggs. However, there's a rare phenomenon called superfetation where another egg is released, fertilized, and attaches to the uterus. The result? Two babies.

100. WILL I BE THE SAME "DOWN THERE?"

Your vagina was made to stretch and make room for a baby's body to come out of. In fact, your pelvic floor muscles can stretch more than three times their usual length (Ashton-Miller & DeLancey, 2009).

The change to your vagina depends on the size of your baby, if there were any complications, and how many babies you already delivered. For the most part, you can do pelvic floor exercises to restore your vagina to its pre-baby glory.

101. I DRANK ALCOHOL BEFORE I KNEW I WAS PREGNANT. WILL THIS HURT MY BABY?

According to the Royal College of Obstetricians and Gynaecologists (n.d), drinking alcohol in the early stages of pregnancy is unlikely to harm your little one. The important thing is that you stop as soon as you find out you're pregnant. That tiny human inside you has a lot of growing to do and you don't want to do anything to hinder their process, especially not when it comes to the development of their brain.

If you feel bad about indulging a little too much before you got the positive pregnancy results, just remember to take your prenatal vitamin, eat healthy food, stay away from undercooked meats, and avoid fish high in mercury. These are all things that will advance your baby's health.

LEAVE A 1-CLICK REVIEW!

I would be incredibly thankful if you could take just 60 seconds to write a brief review on Amazon, even if it's just a couple sentences!

SCAN QR CODE ABOVE OR VISIT LINK BELOW:
http://www.amazon.com/review/create-review?&
asin=B08Y7FHB38&ie

CONCLUSION

Pregnancy causes enormous changes in the human body and with it, comes a not-so-neatly-wrapped bouquet of worries. Often, women are too embarrassed or scared to talk about it. Instead of asking a friend who's been pregnant or discussing it with their doctor, they frantically type away searching for answers on the internet.

It's not easy to grow a baby—you're building a whole new person. Apart from the physical difference, you'll also notice some added anxiety. New mommies will have thousands of questions running through their minds. But that doesn't mean women who've been pregnant before will feel 100% confident about their pregnancy and won't worry at all.

In this book, some serious questions were answered but some hilarious ones too! And I bet that even experienced moms learned a lot from the funny questions new moms often ask. After all, if you're on baby number two, you most probably forgot all about the silly things that crossed your mind the first time.

But I want to get serious for a moment. Your mindset can dramatically affect your pregnancy—it may even steal the joy of this time of your life. If you're overly cautious, you may find yourself focusing on all the things that go wrong, instead of everything that is going right.

One of my clients phoned a pregnancy hotline during her first pregnancy to ask if the pumpkin spice candles she got for thanksgiving would harm her baby. After they reassured her that it's perfectly safe to light one, she still decided against it—just in case. That's taking things a little too far. It's as if she refused to let herself enjoy her pregnancy. When she got pregnant for the second time, everything was different. She focused on doing what she could— eating healthily, avoiding lunch meat and sushi, limiting herself to mild exercise, etc. Basically, she used her common sense and acknowledged that not every twinge she felt meant that something had gone wrong.

Although some anxiety is totally normal during pregnancy—allowing it to prevent you from enjoying this wonderful experience, is not.

Here are some tips to stop anxiety from dimming your pregnancy glow:

Keep a journal. There will be times that you find yourself worrying about something but it isn't an emergency-type question. If this happens, write it down. Before you have to see your doctor or midwife, read through the questions and see if you're still concerned about these things. If you are, then ask the experts! Doctors, nurses, and midwives have heard it all, so you don't have to feel ashamed.

Remind yourself it is okay to enjoy your pregnancy. Denying yourself happiness during this time in your life is not going to make your pregnancy any safer. I know that anxiety is often irrational, but if you keep reassuring yourself that this is a joyous occasion, it will make a big difference. You know what they say: "fake it until you make it."

Trust your gut. You shouldn't dismiss everything that feels wrong as anxiety. That's not a healthy approach either. Instead, assess the situation and if you feel that it is something that should be addressed immediately, then make an appointment with your doctor or go to the emergency room if it is that critical. For example, it is okay to put your mind at ease if you feel your baby moving less than usual or not at all. But once your doctor or midwife established that everything is okay, then move on and focus on the good.

Before I end this book, I want you to take a deep breath right there where you are. Now repeat after me: "I am going to be a good mom." I know that is the one question that has been popping up more times than the rest. I want you to realize that a human's ability to bond is endless; a mother's is even greater. The mere fact that you're concerned about being good enough for your little one shows that you already deeply care for them and they haven't even been born yet!

There you have it expectant mommies—101 answers to your most asked questions. I hope I did what I set out to do and that is to give you enough knowledge to confidently embark on the most amazing nine months of your life.

If you found this book helpful, please leave a favorable review. The more women who read this book, the more stress-free (well, somewhat) pregnancies there will be. Feel free to share it with your friends and family who are expecting a little one themselves.

I wish you a healthy and happy pregnancy!

14 Baby Essentials Every Mom Must Have...

This checklist includes:

- 14 ESSENTIALS THAT YOU DIDN'T KNOW YOU NEEDED FOR YOUR LITTLE ONE AND YOURSELF
- ITEMS WHICH WILL MAKE BEING A MAMA BEAR EASIER
- WHERE YOU CAN PURCHASE THESE ITEMS AT THE LOWEST PRICE

The last thing you want to do is be unprepared and unequipped to give your little one an enjoyable and secure environment to grow up in. It is never too late to prepare for this!

To receive your free Mommy Checklist, visit the link or scan the QR code below:

https://purelypublishing.activehosted.com/f/1

Elizabeth Newbourne is an established nutritionist and loving mother of three. She has devoted her life to helping mothers understand how to take care of themselves and their little ones, both inside the womb during pregnancy and outside, as they guide their newborns through the developmental stages of life.

It is her passion to share with you everything she has learned from bringing into the world her two wonderful boys and her sweet little girl, to her two decades of knowledge in physical and psychological health and nutrition. She has coached and guided countless women through their pregnancies and helped mothers become the best version of themselves for their newborns and families, giving them access to the information she wishes she had when she was a new mother.

Her knowledge as a respected nutritionist, combined with her personal experience as a mother, makes her one of the leading experts on healthy and happy pregnancies and motherhood.

Join the Community:
www.facebook.com/groups/modernsupermom
www.instagram.com/elizabethnewbourne
elizabeth@newbornepublishing.com

REFERENCES

Abu-Ouf, N. M., & Jan, M. M. (2015). The impact of maternal iron deficiency and iron deficiency anemia on child's health. Saudi medical journal, 36(2), 146–149. https://doi.org/10. 15537/smj.2015.2.10289

Addissie, Y.A., Kruszka, P., Troia, A., Wong, Z.C., Everson, J.E., Kozel, B.Z., Lipinski, R.J., Malecki, K.M. & Muenke, M. (2020). Prenatal exposure to pesticides and risk for holoprosencephaly: A case-control study. Environ Health. https://doi.org/10. 1186/s12940-020-00611-z

American College of Obstetricians and Gynecologists. (n.d.). Moderate caffeine consumption during pregnancy. https://www.acog.org/clinical/clinical-

guidance/committee-opinion/articles/2010/08/
moderate-caffeine-consumption-during-pregnancy

American Pregnancy Association. (n.d.). Tattoos during pregnancy. https://americanpregnancy.org/healthy-pregnancy/is-it-safe/tattoos-1178/

American Red Cross. (n.d.) Blood donor eligibility: Alphabetical. https://www.redcrossblood.org/donate-blood/how-to-donate/eligibility-requirements/eligibility-criteria-alphabetical.html

Archibald, A. J., Dolinsky, V. W., & Azad, M. B. (2018). Early-Life Exposure to Non-Nutritive Sweeteners and the Developmental Origins of Childhood Obesity: Global Evidence from Human and Rodent Studies. Nutrients, 10(2), 194. https://doi.org/10.3390/nu10020194

Ashton-Miller, J.A. & DeLancey, J.O. (2009). On the biomechanics of vaginal birth and common sequelae. Annual Review of Biomedical Engineering, 11:1, 163-176. https://www.annualreviews.org/doi/10.1146/annurev-bioeng-061008-124823

Carbone, L., De Vivo, V., Saccone, G., D'Antonio, F., Mercorio, A., Raffone, A., Arduino, B., D'Alessandro, P., Sarno, L., Conforti, A., Maruotti, G.M., Alviggi, C. & Zullo, F. (2019). Sexual intercourse for induction of spontaneous onset of labor: A systematic review and meta-analysis of randomized controlled trials. J Sex Med., 16(11), 1787-1795. https://doi.org/10.1016/j.jsxm.2019.08.002

Centers for Disease Control and Prevention. (n.d.). Toxoplasmosis. https://www.cdc.gov/parasites/toxoplasmosis/index.html#:~:text=More%20than%2040%20million%20men,with%20a%20compromised%20immune%20system

Cho H. (2020). Ambient temperature, birth rate, and birth outcomes: evidence from South Korea. Population and environment, 41(3), 330–346. https://doi.org/10.1007/s11111-019-00333-6

Elton-Marshall, T., Fong, G. T., Zanna, M. P., Jiang, Y., Hammond, D., O'Connor, R. J., Yong, H. H., Li, L., King, B., Li, Q., Borland, R., Cummings, K. M., & Driezen, P. (2010). Beliefs about the relative harm of "light" and "low tar" cigarettes: findings from the International Tobacco Control (ITC) China Survey. Tobacco control, 19 Suppl 2(Suppl_2), i54–i62. https://doi.org/10.1136/tc.2008.029025

Eskenazi, B., Prehn, A.W. & Christianson, R.E. (1995). Passive and active maternal smoking as measured by serum cotinine: the effect on birth-weight. American Journal of Public Health, 85, 395-398. https://doi.org/10.2105/AJPH.85.3.395

Figure 1: Hliznitsova, K. (2020). Woman in pink dress holding purple flower [Photograph]. Unsplash. https://unsplash.com/photos/U89WOwxRRGI/info

Figure 2: Benedit, V. (2020). Sushi on white ceramic plate [Photograph]. Unsplash. https://unsplash.com/photos/-1GEAA8q3wk/info

Figure 3: Peterson, J. (2017). Baby's face [Photograph]. Unsplash. https://unsplash.com/photos/to62zQaH3-o

Figure 4: Johnson, N.E. (2019). Pregnant woman in sunset [Photograph]. Unsplash. https://unsplash.com/photos/iLNKpdIoPzg/info

Figure 5: Vamvouras, A. (2021). Woman in white ceramic bath [Photograph]. Unsplash. https://unsplash.com/photos/faZjI9lIWpU

Figure 6: Reproductive Health Supplies Coalition. (2019). Oral contraceptive pill [Photograph]. Unsplash. https://unsplash.com/photos/gRRtWpFFMK8

Greenop, K.R., Peters, S., Bailey, H.D., Fritschi, L., Attia, J., Scott, R.J., Glass, D.C., de Klerk, N.H., Alvaro, F., Armstrong, B.K. & Milne, E. (2013). Exposure to pesticides and the risk of childhood brain tumors. Cancer Causes Control, 24(7), 1269-78. https://doi.org/10.1007/s10552-013-0205-1

Handel, A. C., Miot, L. D., & Miot, H. A. (2014). Melasma: a clinical and epidemiological review. Anais brasileiros de dermatologia, 89(5), 771–782. https://doi.org/10.1590/abd1806-4841.20143063

Jensen, O.M., Kamby, C. (1982). Intrauterine exposure to saccharin and risk of bladder cancer in man. Int J Cancer, 15;29(5), 507-9. https://doi.org/10.1002/ijc.2910290504

Journal of the American College of Toxicology. (1983). Final report on the safety assessment of Sodium Lauryl Sulfate and Ammonium Lauryl Sulfate. Marry Ann Liebert, Inc., Publishers. https://journals.sagepub.com/doi/pdf/10.3109/10915818309142005

Juhl, M., Strandberg-Larsen, K., Larsen, P.S., Andersen, P.K., Svendsen, S.W., Bonde, J.P. & Nybo Andersen, A.M. (2013). Occupational lifting during pregnancy and risk of fetal death in a large national cohort study. Scand J Work Environ Health, 39(4), 335-42. https://doi.org/10. 5271/sjweh.3335

Kessels R. P. (2003). Patients' memory for medical information. Journal of the Royal Society of Medicine, 96(5), 219–222. https://doi.org/10.1258/jrsm.96.5.219

Ma, J., Shao, H., Lu, X., Zhang, B., & Zhang, G. (2012). Safety and efficacy of airbag midwifery in promoting normal vaginal delivery and reducing caesarean section. Iranian journal of reproductive medicine, 10(6), 595–600

Marnach, M.L., Ramin, K.D., Ramsey, P.S., Song, S.W. & Stensland, J.J. (2003). Characterization of the relationship between joint laxity and maternal hormones in pregnancy. Obstet Gynecol, 101(2), 331-5. https://doi.org/10.1016/s0029-7844(02)02447-x

Prescrire International. (2012). Paracetamol during pregnancy: no particular danger for the child. https://pubmed.ncbi.nlm.nih.gov/22852293/

Royal College of Obstetricians and Gynaecologists. (n.d.). Alcohol and pregnancy [PDF]. https://www.rcog.org.uk/globalassets/documents/patients/

patient-information-leaflets/pregnancy/pi-alcohol-and-pregnancy.pdf

Science Alert. (2018). Here's what happens to your body when you hold in your pee. https://www.sciencealert.com/what-happens-when-you-hold-in-pee-science-2017

Skin Vision. (n.d.). Sun exposure when pregnant. https://www.skinvision.com/articles/sun-exposure-when-pregnant-what-s-important-to-know/#:~:text=Most%20research%20points%20to%20as,the%20body%27s%20vitamin%20D%20needs

Spahn, J.M., Callahan, E.H., Spill, M.K., Wong, Y.P., Benjamin-Neelon, S.E., Birch, L., Black, M.M., Cook, J.T., Faith, M.S., Mennella, J.A. & Casavale, K.O. (2019). Influence of maternal diet on flavor transfer to amniotic fluid and breast milk and children's responses: A systematic review. Am J Clin Nutr, 1;109, 1003S-1026S. https://doi.org/10.1093/ajcn/nqy240

U.S. Department of Health and Human Services. (2006). The health consequences of involuntary exposure to tobacco smoke: A report of the Surgeon General. https://www.hhs.gov/sites/default/files/secondhand-smoke-consumer.pdf

U.S. Department of Health and Human Services. (2010). A report of the Surgeon General: How tobacco smoke causes disease. What it means to you [PDF]. https://www.cdc.gov/tobacco/data_statistics/ sgr/2010/consumer_booklet/pdfs/consumer.pdf

World Health Organization. (n.d.) Who can give blood. https://www.who.int/campaigns/world-blood-donor-day/2018/who-can-give-blood

Printed in Great Britain
by Amazon

77497578R10074